365 Days of Wonder

Best Inspiration Quotes

"Live as if you were to die tomorrow. Learn as if you were to live forever."

— Mahatma Gandhi

"Yesterday is history, tomorrow is a mystery, today is a gift of God, which is why we call it the present."
— Bil Keane

"You have brains in your head. You have feet in your shoes. You can steer yourself any direction you choose. You're on your own. And you know what you know. And YOU are the one who'll decide where to go..."
— Dr. Seuss, Oh, The Places You'll Go!

"It is never too late to be what you might have been."
— Unknown

"There is no greater agony than bearing an untold story inside you."
— Maya Angelou, I Know Why the Caged Bird Sings

"Be yourself; everyone else is already taken."
— Oscar Wilde

"You've gotta dance like there's nobody watching,
Love like you'll never be hurt,
Sing like there's nobody listening,
And live like it's heaven on earth."
— William W. Purkey

"Be the change that you wish to see in the world."
— Mahatma Gandhi

"No one can make you feel inferior without your consent."
— Eleanor Roosevelt, This is My Story

"Live as if you were to die tomorrow. Learn as if you were to live forever."
— Mahatma Gandhi

"Darkness cannot drive out darkness: only light can do that. Hate cannot drive out hate: only love can do that."
— Martin Luther King Jr., A Testament of Hope: The Essential Writings and Speeches

"Without music, life would be a mistake."
— Friedrich Nietzsche, Twilight of the Idols

"We accept the love we think we deserve."
— Stephen Chbosky, The Perks Of Being A Wallflower

"Imperfection is beauty, madness is genius and it's better to be absolutely ridiculous than absolutely boring."
— Marilyn Monroe

"There are only two ways to live your life. One is as though nothing is a miracle. The other is as though everything is a miracle."
— Albert Einstein

"Never doubt that a small group of thoughtful, committed, citizens can change the world. Indeed, it is the only thing that ever has."
— Margaret Mead

"First they ignore you, then they ridicule you, then they fight you, and then you win."
— Mahatma Gandhi

"Two wrongs don't make a right, but they make a good excuse."
— Thomas Szasz

"Whatever you are, be a good one."
— Abraham Lincoln

"Friendship is unnecessary, like philosophy, like art.... It has no survival value; rather it is one of those things which give value to survival."
— C.S. Lewis, The Four Loves

"I hope she'll be a fool -- that's the best thing a girl can be in this world, a beautiful little fool."
— F. Scott Fitzgerald, The Great Gatsby

"Yesterday is history, tomorrow is a mystery, today is a gift of God, which is why we call it the present."
— Bil Keane

"We are all in the gutter, but some of us are looking at the stars."
— Oscar Wilde, Lady Windermere's Fan

"Fairy tales are more than true: not because they tell us that dragons exist, but because they tell us that dragons can be beaten."
— Neil Gaiman, Coraline

"I have not failed. I've just found 10,000 ways that won't work."
— Thomas A. Edison

"The opposite of love is not hate, it's indifference. The opposite of art is not ugliness, it's indifference. The opposite of faith is not heresy, it's indifference. And the opposite of life is not death, it's indifference."
— Elie Wiesel

"I am enough of an artist to draw freely upon my imagination. Imagination is more important than knowledge. Knowledge is limited. Imagination encircles the world."
— Albert Einstein

"I believe that imagination is stronger than knowledge. That myth is more potent than history. That dreams are more powerful than facts. That hope always triumphs over experience. That laughter is the only cure for grief. And I believe that love is stronger than death."
— Robert Fulghum, All I Really Need to Know I Learned in Kindergarten: Uncommon Thoughts On Common Things

"May you live every day of your life."
— Jonathan Swift

"You can't stay in your corner of the Forest waiting for others to come to you. You have to go to them sometimes."
— A.A. Milne, Winnie-the-Pooh

"Isn't it nice to think that tomorrow is a new day with no mistakes in it yet?"
— L.M. Montgomery

"You can talk with someone for years, everyday, and still, it won't mean as much as what you can have when you sit in front of someone, not saying a word, yet you feel that person with your heart, you feel like you have known the person for forever....
connections are made with the heart,
not the tongue."
— C. JoyBell C.

"If my life is going to mean anything, I have to live it myself."
— Rick Riordan, The Lightning Thief

"Always do what you are afraid to do."
— Ralph Waldo Emerson

"When I was 5 years old, my mother always told me that happiness was the key to life. When I went to school, they asked me what I wanted to be when I grew up. I wrote down 'happy'. They told me I didn't understand the assignment, and I told them they didn't understand life."
— John Lennon

"Hope is the thing with feathers
That perches in the soul
And sings the tune without the words
And never stops at all."
— Emily Dickinson

"Our lives begin to end the day we become silent about things that matter."
— Martin Luther King Jr., I Have a Dream: Writings and Speeches That Changed the World

"There is neither happiness nor misery in the world; there is only the comparison of one state with another, nothing more. He who has felt the deepest grief is best able to experience supreme happiness. We must have felt what it is to die, Morrel, that we may appreciate the enjoyments of life.
" Live, then, and be happy, beloved children of my heart, and never forget, that until the day God will deign to reveal the future to man, all human wisdom is contained in these two words, 'Wait and Hope."
— Alexandre Dumas

"In the end, we will remember not the words of our enemies, but the silence of our friends."
— Martin Luther King Jr.

"Do not let your fire go out, spark by irreplaceable spark in the hopeless swamps of the not-quite, the not-yet, and the not-at-all. Do not let the hero in your soul perish in lonely frustration for the life you deserved and have never been able to reach. The world you desire can be won. It exists.. it is real.. it is possible.. it's yours."
— Ayn Rand, Atlas Shrugged

"It is so hard to leave—until you leave. And then it is the easiest goddamned thing in the world."
— John Green, Paper Towns

"Talent hits a target no one else can hit. Genius hits a target no one else can see."
— Arthur Schopenhauer

"He who controls the past controls the future. He who controls the present controls the past."
— George Orwell, 1984

"If you're reading this...
Congratulations, you're alive.
If that's not something to smile about,
then I don't know what is."
— Chad Sugg, Monsters Under Your Head

"The mind is its own place, and in itself can make a heaven of hell, a hell of heaven.."
— John Milton, Paradise Lost

"Waiting is painful. Forgetting is painful. But not knowing which to do is the worst kind of suffering."
― Paulo Coelho, By the River Piedra I Sat Down and Wept

"Pain is inevitable. Suffering is optional."
― Haruki Murakami, What I Talk About When I Talk About Running

"I can be changed by what happens to me. But I refuse to be reduced by it.
(Popular misquote of "You may not control all the events that happen to you, but you can decide not to be reduced by them.")"
― Maya Angelou, Letter to My Daughter

"Fantasy is hardly an escape from reality. It's a way of understanding it."
— Lloyd Alexander

"Do not go where the path may lead, go instead where there is no path and leave a trail."
— Ralph Waldo Emerson

"If you can't fly then run, if you can't run then walk, if you can't walk then crawl, but whatever you do you have to keep moving forward."
— Martin Luther King Jr.

"I love to see a young girl go out and grab the world by the lapels. Life's a bitch. You've got to go out and kick ass."
— Maya Angelou

"The world is indeed full of peril, and in it there are many dark places; but still there is much that is fair, and though in all lands love is now mingled with grief, it grows perhaps the greater."
— J.R.R. Tolkien, The Fellowship of the Ring

"When you have eliminated all which is impossible, then whatever remains, however improbable, must be the truth."
— Arthur Conan Doyle, The Case-Book of Sherlock Holmes

"Turn your wounds into wisdom."
— Oprah Winfrey

"Never let your sense of morals prevent you from doing what is right."
— Isaac Asimov, Foundation

"And, in the end
The love you take
is equal to the love you make."
— Paul McCartney, The Beatles Illustrated Lyrics

"And once the storm is over, you won't remember how you made it through, how you managed to survive. You won't even be sure, whether the storm is really over. But one thing is certain. When you come out of the storm, you won't be the same person who walked in. That's what this storm's all about."
— Haruki Murakami

"What I need is the dandelion in the spring. The bright yellow that means rebirth instead of destruction. The promise that life can go on, no matter how bad our losses. That it can be good again."
— Suzanne Collins, Mockingjay

"Hell is empty and all the devils are here."
— William Shakespeare, The Tempest

"Prayer is not asking. It is a longing of the soul. It is daily admission of one's weakness. It is better in prayer to have a heart without words than words without a heart."
— Mahatma Gandhi

"I am not sure exactly what heaven will be like, but I know that when we die and it comes time for God to judge us, he will not ask, 'How many good things have you done in your life?' rather he will ask, 'How much love did you put into what you did?"
— Mother Teresa

"It isn't what you have or who you are or where you are or what you are doing that makes you happy or unhappy. It is what you think about it."
— Dale Carnegie, How to Win Friends and Influence People

"The future belongs to those who believe in the beauty of their dreams."
— Eleanor Roosevelt

"I like living. I have sometimes been wildly, despairingly, acutely miserable, racked with sorrow; but through it all I still know quite certainly that just to be alive is a grand thing."
— Agatha Christie

"I don't trust people who don't love themselves and tell me, 'I love you.' ... There is an African saying which is: Be careful when a naked person offers you a shirt."
— Maya Angelou

"None but ourselves can free our minds."
— Bob Marley

"War is peace.
Freedom is slavery.
Ignorance is strength."
— George Orwell, 1984

"It is not the critic who counts; not the man who points out how the strong man stumbles, or where the doer of deeds could have done them better. The credit belongs to the man who is actually in the arena, whose face is marred by dust and sweat and blood; who strives valiantly; who errs, who comes short again and again, because there is no effort without error and shortcoming; but who does actually strive to do the deeds; who knows great enthusiasms, the great devotions; who spends himself in a worthy cause; who at the best knows in the end the triumph of high achievement, and who at the worst, if he fails, at least fails while daring greatly, so that his place shall never be with those cold and timid souls who neither know victory nor defeat."
— Theodore Roosevelt

"Don't judge each day by the harvest you reap but by the seeds that you plant."
— Robert Louis Stevenson

"If you remember me, then I don't care if everyone else forgets."
— Haruki Murakami, Kafka on the Shore

"Sometimes our light goes out, but is blown again into instant flame by an encounter with another human being."
— Albert Schweitzer

"Only in the darkness can you see the stars."
— Martin Luther King Jr.

"A woman's heart should be so hidden in God that a man has to seek Him just to find her."
— Max Lucado

"It's kind of fun to do the impossible."
— Walt Disney Company

"When I was a little girl I used to read fairy tales. In fairy tales you meet Prince Charming and he's everything you ever wanted. In fairy tales the bad guy is very easy to spot. The bad guy is always wearing a black cape so you always know who he is. Then you grow up and you realize that Prince Charming is not as easy to find as you thought. You realize the bad guy is not wearing a black cape and he's not easy to spot; he's really funny, and he makes you laugh, and he has perfect hair."
— Taylor Swift

"I do not fear death. I had been dead for billions and billions of years before I was born, and had not suffered the slightest inconvenience from it."
— Mark Twain

"Pain is temporary. Quitting lasts forever."
— Lance Armstrong, Every Second Counts

"The Chinese use two brush strokes to write the word 'crisis.' One brush stroke stands for danger; the other for opportunity. In a crisis, be aware of the danger--but recognize the opportunity."
— John F. Kennedy

"Stories never really end...even if the books like to pretend they do. Stories always go on. They don't end on the last page, any more than they begin on the first page."
— Cornelia Funke, Inkspell

"Simplicity, patience, compassion.
These three are your greatest treasures.
Simple in actions and thoughts, you return to the source of being.
Patient with both friends and enemies,
you accord with the way things are.
Compassionate toward yourself,
you reconcile all beings in the world."
― Lao Tzu, Tao Te Ching

"I was smiling yesterday,I am smiling today and I will smile tomorrow.Simply because life is too short to cry for anything."
― Santosh Kalwar, Quote Me Everyday

"The things you do for yourself are gone when you are gone, but the things you do for others remain as your legacy."
― Kalu Ndukwe Kalu

"The most important kind of freedom is to be what you really are. You trade in your reality for a role. You trade in your sense for an act. You give up your ability to feel, and in exchange, put on a mask. There can't be any large-scale revolution until there's a personal revolution, on an individual level. It's got to happen inside first."
— Jim Morrison

"All the darkness in the world cannot extinguish the light of a single candle."
— Francis of Assisi, The Little Flowers of St. Francis of Assisi

"The secret of health for both mind and body is not to mourn for the past, nor to worry about the future, but to live the present moment wisely and earnestly."
— Bukkyo Dendo Kyokai, The Teaching of Buddha

"The truth is, unless you let go, unless you forgive yourself, unless you forgive the situation, unless you realize that the situation is over, you cannot move forward."
— Steve Maraboli, Unapologetically You: Reflections on Life and the Human Experience

"You never fail until you stop trying."
— Albert Einstein

"You're off to Great Places!
Today is your day!
Your mountain is waiting,
So... get on your way!"
— Dr. Seuss, Oh, The Places You'll Go!

"A painter should begin every canvas with a wash of black, because all things in nature are dark except where exposed by the light."
— Leonardo da Vinci

"People say nothing is impossible, but I do nothing every day."
— A.A. Milne, Winnie-the-Pooh

"Don't say you don't have enough time. You have exactly the same number of hours per day that were given to Helen Keller, Pasteur, Michaelangelo, Mother Teresa, Leonardo da Vinci, Thomas Jefferson, and Albert Einstein."
— H. Jackson Brown Jr.

"Why didn't I learn to treat everything like it was the last time. My greatest regret was how much I believed in the future."
— Jonathan Safran Foer, Extremely Loud and Incredibly Close

"Hope
Smiles from the threshold of the year to come,
Whispering 'it will be happier'..."
— Alfred Tennyson

"If you want to forget something or someone, never hate it, or never hate him/her. Everything and everyone that you hate is engraved upon your heart; if you want to let go of something, if you want to forget, you cannot hate."
— C. JoyBell C.

"One love, one heart, one destiny."
— Bob Marley

"It's not the face, but the expressions on it. It's not the voice, but what you say. It's not how you look in that body, but the thing you do with it. You are beautiful."
— Stephenie Meyer, The Host

"Don't be afraid of your fears. They're not there to scare you. They're there to let you know that something is worth it."
— C. JoyBell C.

"Is 'fat' really the worst thing a human being can be? Is 'fat' worse than 'vindictive', 'jealous', 'shallow', 'vain', 'boring' or 'cruel'? Not to me."
— J.K. Rowling

"Once you have tasted flight, you will forever walk the earth with your eyes turned skyward, for there you have been, and there you will always long to return."
— Leonardo da Vinci

"To see a World in a Grain of Sand
And a Heaven in a Wild Flower,
Hold Infinity in the palm of your hand
And Eternity in an hour."
— William Blake, Auguries of Innocence

"So be sure when you step, Step with care and great tact. And remember that life's A Great Balancing Act. And will you succeed? Yes! You will, indeed! (98 and ¾ percent guaranteed) Kid, you'll move mountains."
— Dr. Seuss, Oh, The Places You'll Go!

"To me, Fearless is not the absense of fear. It's not being completely unafraid. To me, Fearless is having fears. Fearless is having doubts. Lots of them. To me, Fearless is living in spite of those things that scare you to death."
— Taylor Swift

"You see things; you say, 'Why?' But I dream things that never were; and I say 'Why not?"
— George Bernard Shaw, Back to Methuselah

"Clouds come floating into my life, no longer to carry rain or usher storm, but to add color to my sunset sky."
— Rabindranath Tagore, Stray Birds

"The thing about growing up with Fred and George," said Ginny thoughtfully, "is that you sort of start thinking anything's possible if you've got enough nerve."
— J.K. Rowling, Harry Potter and the Half-Blood Prince

"If she's amazing, she won't be easy. If she's easy, she won't be amazing. If she's worth it, you wont give up. If you give up, you're not worthy. ... Truth is, everybody is going to hurt you; you just gotta find the ones worth suffering for."
— Bob Marley, Guitar Chord Songbook - Bob Marley

"Live in the present, remember the past, and fear not the future, for it doesn't exist and never shall. There is only now."
— Christopher Paolini, Eldest

"You is kind. You is smart. You is important."
— Kathryn Stockett, The Help

"Any fool can be happy. It takes a man with real heart to make beauty out of the stuff that makes us weep."
— Clive Barker, Days of Magic, Nights of War

"We have to allow ourselves to be loved by the people who really love us, the people who really matter. Too much of the time, we are blinded by our own pursuits of people to love us, people that don't even matter, while all that time we waste and the people who do love us have to stand on the sidewalk and watch us beg in the streets! It's time to put an end to this. It's time for us to let ourselves be loved."
— C. JoyBell C.

"Start writing, no matter what. The water does not flow until the faucet is turned on."
— Louis L'Amour

"Dance, when you're broken open. Dance, if you've torn the bandage off. Dance in the middle of the fighting. Dance in your blood. Dance when you're perfectly free."
— Jalaluddin Rumi

"Better to be strong than pretty and useless."
— Lilith Saintcrow, Strange Angels

"If you are irritated by every rub, how will your mirror be polished?"
— Jalaluddin Rumi

"The unreal is more powerful than the real. Because nothing is as perfect as you can imagine it. Because its only intangible ideas, concepts, beliefs, fantasies that last. Stone crumbles. Wood rots. People, well, they die. But things as fragile as a thought, a dream, a legend, they can go on and on. If you can change the way people think. The way they see themselves. The way they see the world. You can change the way people live their lives. That's the only lasting thing you can create."
— Chuck Palahniuk, Choke

"Life is a shipwreck, but we must not forget to sing in the lifeboats."
— Voltaire

"It was, he thought, the difference between being dragged into the arena to face a battle to the death and walking into the arena with your head held high. Some people, perhaps, would say that there was little to choose between the two ways, but Dumbledore knew - and so do I, thought Harry, with a rush of fierce pride, and so did my parents - that there was all the difference in the world."
— J.K. Rowling, Harry Potter and the Half-Blood Prince

"You were born with wings, why prefer to crawl through life?"
— Jalaluddin Rumi

"Though nobody can go back and make a new beginning... Anyone can start over and make a new ending."
— Chico Xavier

"Even if you are on the right track, you'll get run over if you just sit there."
— Will Rogers

"We are just an advanced breed of monkeys on a minor planet of a very average star. But we can understand the Universe. That makes us something very special."
— Stephen Hawking

"The most common way people give up their power is by thinking they don't have any."
— Alice Walker

"Understanding is the first step to acceptance, and only with acceptance can there be recovery."
— J.K. Rowling, Harry Potter and the Goblet of Fire

"A ship is safe in harbor, but that's not what ships are for."
— William G.T. Shedd

"You should never be surprised when someone treats you with respect, you should expect it."
— Sarah Dessen, Keeping the Moon

"Maybe everyone can live beyond what they're capable of."
— Markus Zusak, I Am the Messenger

"What makes the desert beautiful,' said the little prince, 'is that somewhere it hides a well...”
— Antoine de Saint-Exupéry, The Little Prince

"Happiness [is] only real when shared"
— Jon Krakauer, Into the Wild

"And in the end it is not the years in your life that count, it's the life in your years."
— Abraham Lincoln

"Try a little harder to be a little better."
— Gordon B. Hinckley

"May the forces of evil become confused on the way to your house."
— George Carlin

"The worst part of success is trying to find someone who is happy for you."
— Bette Midler

"What's the good of living if you don't try a few things?"
— Charles M. Schulz

"The past has no power over the present moment."
— Eckhart Tolle

"Reputation is what other people know about you. Honor is what you know about yourself."
— Lois McMaster Bujold, A Civil Campaign

"There are some things you can't share without ending up liking each other, and knocking out a twelve-foot mountain troll is one of them."
— J.K. Rowling, Harry Potter and the Sorcerer's Stone

"When I was about eight, I decided that the most wonderful thing, next to a human being, was a book."
— Margaret Walker

"I have come to accept the feeling of not knowing where I am going. And I have trained myself to love it. Because it is only when we are suspended in mid-air with no landing in sight, that we force our wings to unravel and alas begin our flight. And as we fly, we still may not know where we are going to. But the miracle is in the unfolding of the wings. You may not know where you're going, but you know that so long as you spread your wings, the winds will carry you."
— C. JoyBell C.

"There was another life that I might have had, but I am having this one."
— Kazuo Ishiguro

"No matter what he does, every person on earth plays a central role in the history of the world. And normally he doesn't know it."
— Paulo Coelho, The Alchemist

"Remember, darkness does not always equate to evil, just as light does not always bring good."
— P.C. Cast, Betrayed

"Nothing in the world is ever completely wrong. Even a stopped clock is right twice a day."
— Paulo Coelho, Brida

"I meant what I said and I said what I meant. An elephant's faithful one-hundred percent!"
— Dr. Seuss, Horton Hatches the Egg

"When people don't express themselves, they die one piece at a time."
— Laurie Halse Anderson, Speak

"Letting go means to come to the realization that some people are a part of your history, but not a part of your destiny."
— Steve Maraboli

"If people refuse to look at you in a new light and they can only see you for what you were, only see you for the mistakes you've made, if they don't realize that you are not your mistakes, then they have to go."
— Steve Maraboli, Life, the Truth, and Being Free

"If you think you are too small to make a difference, try sleeping with a mosquito."
— Dalai Lama XIV

"There must be those among whom we can sit down and weep and still be counted as warriors."
— Adrienne Rich

"Anyone can hide. Facing up to things, working through them, that's what makes you strong."
— Sarah Dessen

"She seems so cool, so focused, so quiet, yet her eyes remain fixed upon the horizon. You think you know all there is to know about her immediately upon meeting her, but everything you think you know is wrong. Passion flows through her like a river of blood. She only looked away for a moment, and the mask slipped, and you fell. All your tomorrows start here."
— Neil Gaiman, Fragile Things: Short Fictions and Wonders

"The only way that we can live, is if we grow. The only way that we can grow is if we change. The only way that we can change is if we learn. The only way we can learn is if we are exposed. And the only way that we can become exposed is if we throw ourselves out into the open. Do it. Throw yourself."
— C. JoyBell C.

"In the end
these things matter most:
How well did you love?
How fully did you live?
How deeply did you let go?"
— Jack Kornfield, Buddha's Little Instruction Book

"Go on with what your heart tells you, or you will lose all."
— Rick Riordan, The Lightning Thief

"The purpose of life is to live it, to taste experience to the utmost, to reach out eagerly and without fear for newer and richer experience."
— Eleanor Roosevelt

"It is the time you have wasted for your rose that makes your rose so important."
— Antoine de Saint-Exupéry, The Little Prince

"What do we live for, if it is not to make life less difficult for each other?"
— George Eliot

"All parents damage their children. It cannot be helped. Youth, like pristine glass, absorbs the prints of its handlers. Some parents smudge, others crack, a few shatter childhoods completely into jagged little pieces, beyond repair."
— Mitch Albom, The Five People You Meet in Heaven

"Change will not come if we wait for some other person, or if we wait for some other time. We are the ones we've been waiting for. We are the change that we seek."
— Barack Obama

"Kindness is a language which the deaf can hear and the blind can see."
— Mark Twain

"When one tugs at a single thing in nature, he finds it attached to the rest of the world."
— John Muir

"I kept always two books in my pocket, one to read, one to write in."
— Robert Louis Stevenson, Essays of Robert Louis Stevenson

"It's not the size of the dog in the fight, it's the size of the fight in the dog."
— Mark Twain

"Lack of direction, not lack of time, is the problem. We all have twenty-four hour days."
— Zig Ziglar

"I will love you always. When this red hair is white, I will still love you. When the smooth softness of youth is replaced by the delicate softness of age, I will still want to touch your skin. When your face is full of the lines of every smile you have ever smiled, of every surprise I have seen flash through your eyes, when every tear you have ever cried has left its mark upon your face, I will treasure you all the more, because I was there to see it all. I will share your life with you, Meredith, and I will love you until the last breath leaves your body or mine."
— Laurell K. Hamilton, A Lick of Frost

"My concern is not whether God is on our side; my greatest concern is to be on God's side, for God is always right."
— Abraham Lincoln

"please believe that things are good with me, and even when they're not, they will be soon enough. And i will always believe the same about you."
— Stephen Chbosky, The Perks Of Being A Wallflower

"Great heroes need great sorrows and burdens, or half their greatness goes unnoticed. It is all part of the fairy tale."
— Peter S. Beagle, The Last Unicorn

"I'd rather be hated for who I am, than loved for who I am not."
— Kurt Cobain

"A woman's heart should be so hidden in God that a man has to seek Him just to find her."
— Maya Angelou

"Trees that are slow to grow bear the best fruit."
— Molière

"Never be bullied into silence. Never allow yourself to be made a victim. Accept no one's definition of your life, but define yourself."
— Harvey Fierstein

"The brick walls are there for a reason. The brick walls are not there to keep us out. The brick walls are there to give us a chance to show how badly we want something. Because the brick walls are there to stop the people who don't want it badly enough. They're there to stop the other people."
— Randy Pausch, The Last Lecture

"What's terrible is to pretend that second-rate is first-rate. To pretend that you don't need love when you do; or you like your work when you know quite well you're capable of better."
— Doris Lessing, The Golden Notebook

"The most beautiful things in the world cannot be seen or touched, they are felt with the heart."
— Antoine de Saint-Exupéry, The Little Prince

"Tears are words that need to be written."
— Paulo Coelho

"Once you have read a book you care about, some part of it is always with you."
— Louis L'Amour, Matagorda/The First Fast Draw

"It does not matter how slowly you go as long as you do not stop."
— Confucius

"Wanting to be someone else is a waste of the person you are."
— Marilyn Monroe

"Every book, every volume you see here, has a soul. The soul of the person who wrote it and of those who read it and lived and dreamed with it. Every time a book changes hands, every time someone runs his eyes down its pages, its spirit grows and strengthens."
— Carlos Ruiz Zafón, The Shadow of the Wind

"So many people walk around with a meaningless life. They seem half-asleep, even when they're busy doing things they think are important. This is because they're chasing the wrong things. The way you get meaning into your life is to devote yourself to loving others, devote yourself to your community around you, and devote yourself to creating something that gives you purpose and meaning."
— Mitch Albom, Tuesdays with Morrie

"Even strength must bow to wisdom sometimes."
— Rick Riordan, The Lightning Thief

"Life is too short to waste any amount of time on wondering what other people think about you. In the first place, if they had better things going on in their lives, they wouldn't have the time to sit around and talk about you. What's important to me is not others' opinions of me, but what's important to me is my opinion of myself."
— C. JoyBell C.

"I wonder how many people don't get the one they want, but end up with the one they're supposed to be with."
— Fannie Flagg, Fried Green Tomatoes at the Whistle Stop Cafe

"Parents can only give good advice or put them on the right paths, but the final forming of a person's character lies in their own hands."
— Anne Frank

"I don't think of all the misery, but of the beauty that still remains."
— Anne Frank, The Diary of a Young Girl

"When things break, it's not the actual breaking that prevents them from getting back together again. It's because a little piece gets lost - the two remaining ends couldn't fit together even if they wanted to. The whole shape has changed."
— John Green, Will Grayson, Will Grayson

"I want to be in a relationship where you telling me you love me is just a ceremonious validation of what you already show me."
— Steve Maraboli, Life, the Truth, and Being Free

"I've been fighting to be who I am all my life. What's the point of being who I am, if I can't have the person who was worth all the fighting for?"
— Stephanie Lennox, I Don't Remember You

"We don't need a list of rights and wrongs, tables of dos and don'ts: we need books, time, and silence. Thou shalt not is soon forgotten, but Once upon a time lasts forever."
— Philip Pullman

"The grand essentials to happiness in this life are something to do, something to love, and something to hope for."
— George Washington Burnap, The Sphere and Duties of Woman: A Course of Lectures

"Do no harm and leave the world a better place than you found it."
— Patricia Cornwell

"However many holy words you read, however many you speak, what good will they do you if you do not act on upon them?"
— Gautama Buddha

"I figured something out. The future is unpredictable."
— John Green, An Abundance of Katherines

"Shoot for the moon. Even if you miss, you'll land among the stars."
— Norman Vincent Peale

"Ask for what you want and be prepared to get it!"
— Maya Angelou

"Whatever you can do or dream you can, begin it. Boldness has genius, power and magic in it!"
— John Anster, The First Part of Goethe's Faust

"Incredible change happens in your life when you decide to take control of what you do have power over instead of craving control over what you don't."
— Steve Maraboli, Life, the Truth, and Being Free

". . . when it comes down to it, that's what life is all about: showing up for the people you love, again and again, until you can't show up anymore."
— Rebecca Walker, Baby Love: Choosing Motherhood After a Lifetime of Ambivalence

"Be steady and well-ordered in your life so that you can be fierce and original in your work."
— Gustave Flaubert

"I've known people that the world has thrown everything at to discourage them...to break their spirit. And yet something about them retains a dignity. They face life and don't ask quarters."
— Horton Foote

"If you don't go after what you want, you'll never have it. If you don't ask, the answer is always no. If you don't step forward, you're always in the same place."
— Nora Roberts

"Others have seen what is and asked why. I have seen what could be and asked why not. "
— Pablo Picasso, Pablo Picasso: Metamorphoses of the Human Form : Graphic Works, 1895-1972

"I must be a mermaid, Rango. I have no fear of depths and a great fear of shallow living."
— Anaïs Nin

"To-morrow, and to-morrow, and to-morrow,
Creeps in this petty pace from day to day,
To the last syllable of recorded time;
And all our yesterdays have lighted fools
The way to dusty death. Out, out, brief candle!
Life's but a walking shadow, a poor player,
That struts and frets his hour upon the stage,
And then is heard no more. It is a tale
Told by an idiot, full of sound and fury,
Signifying nothing."
— William Shakespeare, Macbeth

"I sought to hear the voice of God and climbed the topmost steeple, but God declared: "Go down again - I dwell among the people."
— John Henry Newman

"If we listened to our intellect we'd never have a love affair. We'd never have a friendship. We'd never go in business because we'd be cynical: "It's gonna go wrong." Or "She's going to hurt me." Or,"I've had a couple of bad love affairs, so therefore . . ." Well, that's nonsense. You're going to miss life. You've got to jump off the cliff all the time and build your wings on the way down."
— Ray Bradbury

"Only people who are capable of loving strongly can also suffer great sorrow, but this same necessity of loving serves to counteract their grief and heals them."
— Leo Tolstoy

"The question is not what you look at, but what you see."
— Henry David Thoreau

"The starting point of all achievement is DESIRE. Keep this constantly in mind. Weak desire brings weak results, just as a small fire makes a small amount of heat."
— Napoleon Hill, Think and Grow Rich

"All thinking men are atheists."
— Ernest Hemingway, A Farewell to Arms

"I am a part of all that I have met."
— Alfred Tennyson, The Complete Poetical Works of Tennyson

"A man who dares to waste one hour of time has not discovered the value of life."
— Charles Darwin, The Life & Letters of Charles Darwin

"There is nothing more dreadful than the habit of doubt. Doubt separates people. It is a poison that disintegrates friendships and breaks up pleasant relations. It is a thorn that irritates and hurts; it is a sword that kills."
— Gautama Buddha

"We never know the quality of someone else's life, though we seldom resist the temptation to assume and pass judgement."
— Tami Hoag, Dark Horse

"Courage isn't having the strength to go on - it is going on when you don't have strength."
— Napoléon Bonaparte

"If you want to be happy, be."
— Leo Tolstoy

"Whatever you do, you need courage. Whatever course you decide upon, there is always someone to tell you that you are wrong. There are always difficulties arising that tempt you to believe your critics are right. To map out a course of action and follow it to an end requires some of the same courage that a soldier needs. Peace has its victories, but it takes brave men and women to win them."
— Ralph Waldo Emerson

"If we have no peace, it is because we have forgotten that we belong to each other."
— Mother Teresa

"I just want you to know that you're very special… and the only reason I'm telling you is that I don't know if anyone else ever has."
— Stephen Chbosky, The Perks Of Being A Wallflower

"A concept is a brick. It can be used to build a courthouse of reason. Or it can be thrown through the window."
— Gilles Deleuze, A Thousand Plateaus: Capitalism and Schizophrenia

"The desire to reach for the stars is ambitious. The desire to reach hearts is wise."
— Maya Angelou

"Stepping onto a brand-new path is difficult, but not more difficult than remaining in a situation, which is not nurturing to the whole woman."
— Maya Angelou

"No matter how plain a woman may be, if truth and honesty are written across her face, she will be beautiful."
— Eleanor Roosevelt

"Keep your face always toward the sunshine - and shadows will fall behind you."
― Walt Whitman

"I have never met a man so ignorant that I couldn't learn something from him."
― Galileo Galilei

"My only advice is to stay aware, listen carefully, and yell for help if you need it."
― Judy Blume

"It is easy in the world to live after the world's opinion; it is easy in solitude to live after our own; but the great man is he who in the midst of the crowd keeps with perfect sweetness the independence of solitude."
— Ralph Waldo Emerson, The Complete Prose Works of Ralph Waldo Emerson

"No matter how your heart is grieving, if you keep on believing, the dreams that you wish will come true."
— Walt Disney Company

"The real heroes anyway aren't the people doing things; the real heroes are the people NOTICING things, paying attention."
— John Green, The Fault in Our Stars

"The unhappiest people in this world, are those who care the most about what other people think."
— C. JoyBell C.

"Jane, be still; don't struggle so like a wild, frantic bird, that is rending its own plumage in its desperation."
"I am no bird; and no net ensnares me; I am a free human being, with an independent will; which I now exert to leave you."
— Charlotte Brontë, Jane Eyre

"Earth provides enough to satisfy every man's needs, but not every man's greed."
— Mahatma Gandhi

"We're so self-important. So arrogant. Everybody's going to save something now. Save the trees, save the bees, save the whales, save the snails. And the supreme arrogance? Save the planet! Are these people kidding? Save the planet? We don't even know how to take care of ourselves; we haven't learned how to care for one another. We're gonna save the fuckin' planet? . . . And, by the way, there's nothing wrong with the planet in the first place. The planet is fine. The people are fucked! Compared with the people, the planet is doin' great. It's been here over four billion years . . . The planet isn't goin' anywhere, folks. We are! We're goin' away. Pack your shit, we're goin' away. And we won't leave much of a trace. Thank God for that. Nothing left. Maybe a little Styrofoam. The planet will be here, and we'll be gone. Another failed mutation; another closed-end biological mistake."
— George Carlin

"Two roads diverged in a wood, and I -
I took the one less traveled by,
And that has made all the difference."
— Robert Frost

"Imagination is everything. It is the preview of life's coming attractions."
— Albert Einstein

"If you make a mistake and do not correct it, this is called a mistake."
— Confucius

"You might as well answer the door, my child,
the truth is furiously knocking."
— Lucille Clifton, Good Woman: Poems and a Memoir 1969-1980

"Pain is a pesky part of being human, I've learned it feels like a stab wound to the heart, something I wish we could all do without, in our lives here. Pain is a sudden hurt that can't be escaped. But then I have also learned that because of pain, I can feel the beauty, tenderness, and freedom of healing. Pain feels like a fast stab wound to the heart. But then healing feels like the wind against your face when you are spreading your wings and flying through the air! We may not have wings growing out of our backs, but healing is the closest thing that will give us that wind against our faces."
— C. JoyBell C.

"Just because you can doesn't mean you should."
— Sherrilyn Kenyon

"Don't let the bastards grind you down."
— Margaret Atwood, The Handmaid's Tale

"We are flawed creatures, all of us. Some of us think that means we should fix our flaws. But get rid of my flaws and there would be no one left."
— Sarah Vowell, Take the Cannoli

"Any book that helps a child to form a habit of reading, to make reading one of his deep and continuing needs, is good for him."
— Maya Angelou

"Write it on your heart that every day is the best day in the year."
— Ralph Waldo Emerson

"I am not a teacher, but an awakener."
— Robert Frost

"True love is not so much a matter of romance as it is a matter of anxious concern for the well-being of one's companion."
— Gordon B. Hinckley, Stand a Little Taller

"Have courage for the great sorrows of life and patience for the small ones; and when you have laboriously accomplished your daily task, go to sleep in peace. God is awake."
— Victor Hugo

"why are trying so hard to fit in, when you're born to stand out"
— Oliver James

"Men are from Earth, women are from Earth. Deal with it."
— George Carlin

"Because paper has more patience than people. "
— Anne Frank

"The best thing to hold onto in life is each other."
— Audrey Hepburn

"Happiness is not the absence of problems, it's the ability to deal with them."
— Steve Maraboli, Life, the Truth, and Being Free

"Well, we all make mistakes, dear, so just put it behind you. We should regret our mistakes and learn from them, but never carry them forward into the future with us."
— L.M. Montgomery, Anne of Avonlea

"Sometimes life knocks you on your ass... get up, get up, get up!!! Happiness is not the absence of problems, it's the ability to deal with them."
— Steve Maraboli, Life, the Truth, and Being Free

"To love and win is the best thing.
To love and lose, the next best."
— William Makepeace Thackeray

"The heart is the toughest part of the body.
Tenderness is in the hands."
— Carolyn Forché, The Country Between Us

"Because,' she said, 'when you're scared but you still do it anyway, that's brave."
— Neil Gaiman, Coraline

"Happiness is like a butterfly which, when pursued, is always beyond our grasp, but, if you will sit down quietly, may alight upon you."
— Nathaniel Hawthorne

"Sometimes God allows what he hates to accomplish what he loves."
— Joni Eareckson Tada, The God I Love

"We don't make mistakes, just happy little accidents."
— Bob Ross

"Where there is ruin, there is hope for a treasure."
— Jalaluddin Rumi

"Not being heard is no reason for silence."
― Victor Hugo, Les Misérables

"Hearts are breakable," Isabelle said. "And I think even when you heal, you're never what you were before"."
― Cassandra Clare, City of Fallen Angels

"If you want to be happy, do not dwell in the past, do not worry about the future, focus on living fully in the present."
― Roy T. Bennett, The Light in the Heart

"Spoon feeding in the long run teaches us nothing but the shape of the spoon."
— E.M. Forster

"Only after disaster can we be resurrected. It's only after you've lost everything that you're free to do anything. Nothing is static, everything is evolving, everything is falling apart."
— Chuck Palahniuk, Fight Club

"Dear God," she prayed, "let me be something every minute of every hour of my life. Let me be gay; let me be sad. Let me be cold; let me be warm. Let me be hungry...have too much to eat. Let me be ragged or well dressed. Let me be sincere - be deceitful. Let me be truthful; let me be a liar. Let me be honorable and let me sin. Only let me be something every blessed minute. And when I sleep, let me dream all the time so that not one little piece of living is ever lost."
— Betty Smith, A Tree Grows in Brooklyn

"There is a candle in your heart, ready to be kindled.
There is a void in your soul, ready to be filled.
You feel it, don't you?"
— Jalaluddin Rumi

"Shoot for the moon, even if you fail, you'll land among the stars"
— Cecelia Ahern, P.S. I Love You

"A star falls from the sky and into your hands. Then it seeps through your veins and swims inside your blood and becomes every part of you. And then you have to put it back into the sky. And it's the most painful thing you'll ever have to do and that you've ever done. But what's yours is yours. Whether it's up in the sky or here in your hands. And one day, it'll fall from the sky and hit you in the head real hard and that time, you won't have to put it back in the sky again."
— C. JoyBell C.

"When I let go of what I am, I become what I might be."
— Lao Tzu

"How would your life be different if…You stopped making negative judgmental assumptions about people you encounter? Let today be the day…You look for the good in everyone you meet and respect their journey."
— Steve Maraboli, Life, the Truth, and Being Free

"You may tell a tale that takes up residence in someone's soul, becomes their blood and self and purpose. That tale will move them and drive them and who knows that they might do because of it, because of your words. That is your role, your gift."
— Erin Morgenstern, The Night Circus

"All that we are is the result of what we have thought: it is founded on our thoughts and made up of our thoughts. If a man speak or act with an evil thought, suffering follows him as the wheel follows the hoof of the beast that draws the wagon.... If a man speak or act with a good thought, happiness follows him like a shadow that never leaves him."
— Gautama Buddha

"For me, I am driven by two main philosophies: know more today about the world than I knew yesterday and lessen the suffering of others. You'd be surprised how far that gets you."
— Neil deGrasse Tyson

"I never want to change so much that people can't recognize me."
— Taylor Swift

"God allows us to experience the low points of life in order to teach us lessons that we could learn in no other way."
— C.S. Lewis

"I must be willing to give up what I am in order to become what I will be."
— Albert Einstein

"The reason birds can fly and we can't is simply because they have perfect faith, for to have faith is to have wings."
— J.M. Barrie, The Little White Bird

"In the name of God, stop a moment, cease your work, look around you."
— Leo Tolstoy

"Life sucks, and then you die..."
— Stephenie Meyer, Breaking Dawn

"You'll never find a rainbow if you're looking down"
— Charlie Chaplin

"Death is no more than passing from one room into another. But there's a difference for me, you know. Because in that other room I shall be able to see."
— Helen Keller

"He that can have patience can have what he will."
— Benjamin Franklin

"Don't be afraid of enemies who attack you. Be afraid of the friends who flatter you."
— Dale Carnegie, How to Win Friends and Influence People

"Above all else, guard your heart for it affects everything else you do."
— Anonymous, Holy Bible: New International Version

"The biggest adventure you can ever take is to live the life of your dreams."
— Oprah Winfrey

"Everything can be taken from a man but one thing: the last of the human freedoms—to choose one's attitude in any given set of circumstances, to choose one's own way."
— Viktor E. Frankl, Man's Search for Meaning

"There is no good and evil, there is only power and those too weak to seek it."
— J.K. Rowling, Harry Potter and the Sorcerer's Stone

"You only need one man to love you. But him to love you free like a wildfire, crazy like the moon, always like tomorrow, sudden like an inhale and overcoming like the tides. Only one man and all of this."
— C. JoyBell C.

"Wanting to be someone else is a waste of who you are"
— Kurt Cobain

"No one really knows why they are alive until they know what they'd die for."
— Martin Luther King Jr.

"Everybody is special. Everybody. Everybody is a hero, a lover, a fool, a villain. Everybody. Everybody has their story to tell."
— Alan Moore, V for Vendetta

"Swords can win territories but not hearts, forces can bend heads but not minds."
— Mirza Tahir Ahmad

"The only person who can pull me down is myself, and I'm not going to let myself pull me down anymore."
— C. JoyBell C.

"The higher we soar the smaller we appear to those who cannot fly."
— Friedrich Nietzsche, Thus Spoke Zarathustra

"You're beautiful, but you're empty...One couldn't die for you. Of course, an ordinary passerby would think my rose looked just like you. But my rose, all on her own, is more important than all of you together, since she's the one I've watered. Since she's the one I put under glass, since she's the one I sheltered behind the screen. Since she's the one for whom I killed the caterpillars (except the two or three butterflies). Since she's the one I listened to when she complained, or when she boasted, or even sometimes when she said nothing at all. Since she's my rose."
— Antoine de Saint-Exupéry, The Little Prince

"Change the way you look at things and the things you look at change."
— Wayne W. Dyer

"Death is not the greatest loss in life. The greatest loss is what dies inside while still alive. Never surrender."
— Tupac Shakur

"I live my life in widening circles that reach out across the world."
— Rainer Maria Rilke, Rilke's Book of Hours: Love Poems to God

"Aim higher in case you fall short."
— Suzanne Collins, Catching Fire

"A Penny Saved is a Penny Earned"
— Benjamin Franklin

"In the end you should always do the right thing even if it's hard."
— Nicholas Sparks, The Last Song

"Every day, think as you wake up, today I am fortunate to be alive, I have a precious human life, I am not going to waste it. I am going to use all my energies to develop myself, to expand my heart out to others; to achieve enlightenment for the benefit of all beings. I am going to have kind thoughts towards others, I am not going to get angry or think badly about others. I am going to benefit others as much as I can."
— Dalai Lama XIV

"Do not seek the because - in love there is no because, no reason, no explanation, no solutions."
— Anaïs Nin, Henry And June

"The damage was permanent; there would always be scars. But even the angriest scars faded over time until it was difficult to see them written on the skin at all, and the only thing that remained was the memory of how painful it had been."
— Jodi Picoult

"I think that we are like stars. Something happens to burst us open; but when we burst open and think we are dying; we're actually turning into a supernova. And then when we look at ourselves again, we see that we're suddenly more beautiful than we ever were before!"
— C. JoyBell C.

"Excellence is never an accident. It is always the result of high intention, sincere effort, and intelligent execution; it represents the wise choice of many alternatives - choice, not chance, determines your destiny."
— Aristotle

"Dumbledore will only leave from Hogwarts when there are none loyal to him!"
— J.K. Rowling, Harry Potter and the Half-Blood Prince

"Many of life's failures are people who did not realize how close they were to success when they gave up."
— Thomas A. Edison

"Make the most of yourself....for that is all there is of you."
— Ralph Waldo Emerson

"We meet no ordinary people in our lives."
— C.S. Lewis

"Around here, however, we don't look backwards for very long. We keep moving forward, opening up new doors and doing new things, because we're curious...and curiosity keeps leading us down new paths."
— Walt Disney Company

"There's so much to be grateful for, words are poor things."
— Marilynne Robinson, Home

"We travel, some of us forever, to seek other states, other lives, other souls."
— Anaïs Nin, The Diary of Anaïs Nin, Vol. 7: 1966-1974

"If a man is called to be a street sweeper, he should sweep streets even as a Michaelangelo painted, or Beethoven composed music or Shakespeare wrote poetry. He should sweep streets so well that all the hosts of heaven and earth will pause to say, 'Here lived a great street sweeper who did his job well."
— Martin Luther King Jr.

"The best things in life make you sweaty."
— Edgar Allan Poe

"Believe you can and you're halfway there."
— Theodore Roosevelt

"For like a shaft, clear and cold, the thought pierced him that in the end the Shadow was only a small and passing thing: there was light and high beauty for ever beyond its reach."
— J.R.R. Tolkien, The Return of the King

"There is nothing more rare, nor more beautiful, than a woman being unapologetically herself; comfortable in her perfect imperfection. To me, that is the true essence of beauty."
— Steve Maraboli, Unapologetically You: Reflections on Life and the Human Experience

"Every man is a damn fool for at least five minutes every day; wisdom consists in not exceeding the limit."
— Elbert Hubbard, The Roycroft Dictionary Concocted by Ali Baba and the Bunch on Rainy Days

"It's okay," he said. "We're together." He didn't say you're okay, or we're alive. After all they'd been through over the last year, he knew that the most important thing was that they were together. She loved him for saying that."
— Rick Riordan, The Mark of Athena

"Music melts all the separate parts of our bodies together."
— Anaïs Nin

"Be empty of worrying.
Think of who created thought!

Why do you stay in prison
When the door is so wide open?"
— Jalaluddin Rumi, The Essential Rumi

"I'd rather learn from one bird how to sing
than teach ten thousand stars how not to dance"
— E.E. Cummings

"Believe in Your Heart
Believe in your heart that you're meant to live a life full of passion,
purpose, magic and miracles."
— Roy T. Bennett, The Light in the Heart

"There is the great lesson of 'Beauty and the Beast,' that a thing
must be loved before it is lovable."
— G.K. Chesterton

"There are two ways to reach me: by way of kisses or by way of the imagination. But there is a hierarchy: the kisses alone don't work."
— Anaïs Nin, Henry And June

"Nothing great was ever achieved without enthusiasm."
— Ralph Waldo Emerson

"Dream as if you will live forever; Live as if you will die today."
— James Dean

"I said to my soul, be still and wait without hope, for hope would be hope for the wrong thing; wait without love, for love would be love of the wrong thing; there is yet faith, but the faith and the love are all in the waiting. Wait without thought, for you are not ready for thought: So the darkness shall be the light, and the stillness the dancing."
— T.S. Eliot

"Owning our story can be hard but not nearly as difficult as spending our lives running from it. Embracing our vulnerabilities is risky but not nearly as dangerous as giving up on love and belonging and joy—the experiences that make us the most vulnerable. Only when we are brave enough to explore the darkness will we discover the infinite power of our light."
— Brené Brown

"It is always the false that makes you suffer, the false desires and fears, the false values and ideas, the false relationships between people. Abandon the false and you are free of pain; truth makes happy, truth liberates."
— Nisargadatta Maharaj

"Travel far enough, you meet yourself."
— David Mitchell, Cloud Atlas

"Fiction is art and art is the triumph over chaos… to celebrate a world that lies spread out around us like a bewildering and stupendous dream."
— John Cheever

"We are products of our past, but we don't have to be prisoners of it."
— Rick Warren, The Purpose Driven Life: What on Earth Am I Here for?

"Too often we underestimate the power of a touch, a smile, a kind word, a listening ear, an honest compliment, or the smallest act of caring, all of which have the potential to turn a life around."
— Leo Buscaglia

"What are you going to do with your life?" In one way or another it seemed that people had been asking her this forever; teachers, her parents, friends at three in the morning, but the question had never seemed this pressing and still she was no nearer an answer... "Live each day as if it's your last', that was the conventional advice, but really, who had the energy for that? What if it rained or you felt a bit glandy? It just wasn't practical. Better by far to be good and courageous and bold and to make difference. Not change the world exactly, but the bit around you. Cherish your friends, stay true to your principles, live passionately and fully and well. Experience new things. Love and be loved, if you ever get the chance."
— David Nicholls, One Day

"I shall look at you out of the corner of my eye, and you will say nothing. Words are the source of misunderstandings."
— Antoine de Saint-Exupéry

"If you are lazy, and accept your lot, you may live in it. If you are willing to work, you can write your name anywhere you choose."
— Gene Stratton-Porter, A Girl of the Limberlost

"Everything you can imagine is real."
— Pablo Picasso

"You can never get a cup of tea large enough or a book long enough to suit me."
— C.S. Lewis

"To the well-organized mind, death is but the next great adventure."
— J.K. Rowling, Harry Potter and the Sorcerer's Stone

"Life isn't about finding yourself. Life is about creating yourself."
— George Bernard Shaw

"Do what you can, with what you have, where you are."
— Theodore Roosevelt

"Listen to the mustn'ts, child. Listen to the don'ts. Listen to the shouldn'ts, the impossibles, the won'ts. Listen to the never haves, then listen close to me... Anything can happen, child. Anything can be."
— Shel Silverstein

"When one door of happiness closes, another opens; but often we look so long at the closed door that we do not see the one which has been opened for us."
— Helen Keller

"Success is not final, failure is not fatal: it is the courage to continue that counts."
— Winston S. Churchill

"So, this is my life. And I want you to know that I am both happy and sad and I'm still trying to figure out how that could be."
— Stephen Chbosky, The Perks Of Being A Wallflower

"You may say I'm a dreamer, but I'm not the only one. I hope someday you'll join us. And the world will live as one."
— John Lennon

"And, when you want something, all the universe conspires in helping you to achieve it."
— Paulo Coelho, The Alchemist

"It's no use going back to yesterday, because I was a different person then."
— Lewis Carroll, Alice in Wonderland

"What you're supposed to do when you don't like a thing is change it. If you can't change it, change the way you think about it. Don't complain."
— Maya Angelou, Wouldn't Take Nothing for My Journey Now

"A person's a person, no matter how small."
— Dr. Seuss, Horton Hears a Who!

"He's not perfect. You aren't either, and the two of you will never be perfect. But if he can make you laugh at least once, causes you to think twice, and if he admits to being human and making mistakes, hold onto him and give him the most you can. He isn't going to quote poetry, he's not thinking about you every moment, but he will give you a part of him that he knows you could break. Don't hurt him, don't change him, and don't expect for more than he can give. Don't analyze. Smile when he makes you happy, yell when he makes you mad, and miss him when he's not there. Love hard when there is love to be had. Because perfect guys don't exist, but there's always one guy that is perfect for you."
— Bob Marley

"It's the possibility of having a dream come true that makes life interesting."
— Paulo Coelho, The Alchemist

"You can't live your life for other people. You've got to do what's right for you, even if it hurts some people you love."
— Nicholas Sparks, The Notebook

"When we honestly ask ourselves which person in our lives mean the most to us, we often find that it is those who, instead of giving advice, solutions, or cures, have chosen rather to share our pain and touch our wounds with a warm and tender hand. The friend who can be silent with us in a moment of despair or confusion, who can stay with us in an hour of grief and bereavement, who can tolerate not knowing, not curing, not healing and face with us the reality of our powerlessness, that is a friend who cares."
— Henri J.M. Nouwen, Out of Solitude: Three Meditations on the Christian Life

"Well-behaved women seldom make history."
— Laurel Thatcher Ulrich, Well-Behaved Women Seldom Make History

"Nothing is impossible, the word itself says 'I'm possible'!"
— Audrey Hepburn

"When I despair, I remember that all through history the way of truth and love have always won. There have been tyrants and murderers, and for a time, they can seem invincible, but in the end, they always fall. Think of it--always."
— Mahatma Gandhi

"I can't give you a sure-fire formula for success, but I can give you a formula for failure: try to please everybody all the time."
— Herbert Bayard Swope

"Do what you feel in your heart to be right — for you'll be criticized anyway."
— Eleanor Roosevelt

"[...]the only people for me are the mad ones, the ones who are mad to live, mad to talk, mad to be saved, desirous of everything at the same time, the ones who never yawn or say a commonplace thing, but burn, burn, burn like fabulous yellow roman candles exploding like spiders across the stars and in the middle you see the blue centerlight pop and everybody goes "Awww!"
— Jack Kerouac, On the Road

"Happiness is not something ready made. It comes from your own actions."
— Dalai Lama XIV

"Peace begins with a smile.."
— Mother Teresa

"Imagining the future is a kind of nostalgia. (...) You spend your whole life stuck in the labyrinth, thinking about how you'll escape it one day, and how awesome it will be, and imagining that future keeps you going, but you never do it. You just use the future to escape the present."
— John Green, Looking for Alaska

"So we beat on, boats against the current, borne back ceaselessly into the past."
— F. Scott Fitzgerald, The Great Gatsby

"Do not read, as children do, to amuse yourself, or like the ambitious, for the purpose of instruction. No, read in order to live."
— Gustave Flaubert

"What lies behind us and what lies before us are tiny matters compared to what lies within us."
— Ralph Waldo Emerson

Thank you

Printed in Poland
by Amazon Fulfillment
Poland Sp. z o.o., Wrocław